CONTENTS

KT-529-090

Cutting a Record SCOUTING FOR GIRLS 6

Record Labels MCFLY 8

Managers LOUIS WALSH 10

Manufactured Band THE SATURDAYS 12

Raw Talent N-DUBZ 14

Instant Hit THE WANTED 16

Reality Shows JLS 18

Comeback Kings TAKE THAT 20

Changing Faces SUGABABES 22

Festivals BIFFY CLYRO 24

Rock Megastars MUSE 26

Glossary and Further Information 28

Index 30

Words in **bold** are in the glossary.

SCOUTING FOR GIRLS

Lots of people join bands and dream of fame, fortune and a devoted following of screaming fans. Only the best pop bands make it into the charts and get to live the dream. The key to success is having great songs and a unique sound.

SFG members Greg Churchouse, Roy Stride and Pete Ellard (left to right) pose for photos before performing at the O2 Arena in London.

MAKING MUSIC

Making a record is a tricky business. Singles must be filled with catchy **hooks** that stand out and make listeners remember the song. Chart-topping band Scouting for Girls (SFG) have proven to be masters at this, with singles including 'It's Not About You' and 'She's So Lovely'. The rest of the tracks on an album have to be almost as good (if not as good) and different enough to keep the listener interested.

DEBUT ALBUM

SFG played local **gigs** and built up a **fan base** on the Internet through websites such as Myspace and Pulse Rated. Once they got signed, they recorded their self-titled **debut** album at Helioscentric Studios in East Sussex. SFG worked with **record** **producer** Andy Green, who has produced tracks for Keane, Duffy and Paolo Nutini. Their album *Scouting for Girls* was a massive success and has sold nearly a million copies.

THE TRICKY FOLLOW-UP ALBUM

Making a second album can be a daunting task for bands, as they try to create a fresh sound that will still appeal to their fan base. SFG spent a year working hard in the studio to make their second album. They chose to keep the basics of what their fans love – big hooks, singalong anthems and a party **vibe** – but give the album a more grown-up sound. It proved to be as popular as the first, with the debut single shooting straight to Number One in the charts.

'We wanted to write the perfect pop song and an album where every song was good enough to be a single.'

ROY STRIDE (LEAD SINGER)

CELEB POP BANDS

LAURA DURMAN

W

FRANKLIN WATTS

LONDON • SYDNEY

First published in 2011 by Franklin Watts
338 Euston Road
London NW1 3BH

Franklin Watts Australia
Level 17/207 Kent Street
Sydney NSW 2000

© 2011 Franklin Watts

ISBN: 978 1 4451 0532 1

Dewey classification number: 782.4'2166

A CIP catalogue record for this book is available from the British Library.

Planning and production by Discovery Books Limited
Editor: Laura Durman
Designer: D.R. ink

Printed in China

Franklin Watts is a division of Hachette Children's Books, an Hachette UK company.
www.hachette.co.uk

Photo acknowledgements: Getty Images: pp. 3 and 12–13 (Simone Joyner/Stringer),
6–7 (Claire R Greenway), 7 (Harry Herd), 10 (Dave Hogan/Stringer), 11 (M J Kim),
14 and 29 (Dave Hogan/Stringer), 16–17 (Dave Hogan/Stringer), 16 (Shirlaine Forrest),
20 (Tim Roney), 21 (Dave Hogan/Stringer), 22 (Samir Hussein), 24 (Brian Sweeney),
25 (Barney Britton), 26 (Martin Philbey/Redferns), 27 (Bernd Mueller/Redferns); Rex
Features: pp. 8–9 (Geoffrey Swaine), 18–19 (Terry Harris), 23; Shutterstock: pp. 5, 19
(worldswildlifewonders).

Cover photos: Getty Images: JLS (Dave Hogan/Stringer), N-Dubz (Jon Furniss).

To the best of its knowledge, the Publisher believes the facts in this book to be true at the
time of going to press. However, due to the nature of celebrity, it is impossible to guarantee
that all the facts will still be current at the time of reading.

SFG perform to their adoring fans in Bournemouth.

CELEB BIO

Roy Stride (lead singer)

Date of birth **27 September 1978**

Place of birth **London, UK**

Albums *Scouting for Girls* (2007), *Everybody Wants to Be on TV* (2010)

Achievements **Knocking Lady Gaga off the top spot with their first Number One single 'This Ain't a Love Song'**

MCFLY

Getting a record contract is the ultimate goal of any wannabe pop star. **Record labels** should provide guidance and promotion for the artists they have signed. But sometimes having a record contract isn't as brilliant as it seems…

THE BASICS

Record labels sign artists and bands that they think will be successful and make them money. Artists often have to approach many labels before they are offered a contract. Record boss Simon Cowell famously turned down the Spice Girls who became the most successful girl band of all time! However, some bands, such as McFly, find a different route into a record contract.

EARLY MCFLY

Tom Fletcher was invited to join a songwriting project for pop band Busted at Island Records (part of the Universal Records group). When Danny Jones **auditioned** for an Island Records boy band, Fletcher spotted him and was impressed by his musical talent. The two began working together and **recruited** guitarist Dougie Poynter and drummer Harry Judd. The newly-formed band persuaded Island Records to sign them.

GOING FULL CIRCLE

In true rock 'n' roll style, McFly quit Island Records in 2007 because they were unhappy with decisions the label had made. The lads set up their own label, Super Records, and released their *Radio:Active* album which reached Number One. Having proved their talent and worth, McFly returned to Universal Records and signed a deal giving McFly a 50/50 split of control over all decisions about the band. With the label's backing they launched the Super City website which gives fans a unique insight into the band's lives.

The members of McFly (left to right): Dougie Poynter (bass guitar), Tom Fletcher (lead vocals and guitar), Harry Judd (drums) and Danny Jones (lead vocals and guitar).

McFly launched their Super City website in 2010 with backing from Universal Records.

CELEB BIO

Date of birth Tom Fletcher (vocals and guitar) 17 July 1985, Harry Judd (drums) 23 December 1985, Danny Jones (vocals and guitar) 12 March 1986, Dougie Poynter (bass guitar) 30 November 1987

Place of birth London, Bolton and Essex, UK

Albums *Room on the 3rd Floor* (2004), *Wonderland* (2005), *Motion in the Ocean* (2006), *Radio:Active* (2008), *Above the Noise* (2010)

Achievements Nine Smash Hits Awards and one Brit Award

'[Now] there's no competition between what we want and what the label wants and it's even for everyone involved.' DANNY JONES

supercity.mcfly.com *And, if you like this… check out Olly Murs* www.ollymurs.com *and Jonas Brothers* www.jonasbrothers.com

LOUIS WALSH

Bands are good at being creative and coming up with great songs. But they usually need someone else to handle the business side of things. This is where the band manager comes in.

BOYZONE BEGINNINGS

The manager's job is to **negotiate** deals and contracts for the band and make sure they are being looked after. One of the most successful pop band managers is Irishman Louis Walsh. Having seen the success of Take That, Louis advertised for members of an Irish boy band. Boyzone was created in 1993 and achieved international success, selling 12 million records worldwide. They reformed in 2007, once again under the management of Walsh.

BOY BAND VS GIRL BAND

Walsh used the same **formula** to create another Irish boy band in the late 1990s – Westlife. Walsh then appeared on television as a judge in the show *Popstars: The Rivals*. In the show, five contestants were chosen to form the girl group Girls Aloud. After the competition Walsh managed Girls Aloud and their debut single reached Number One and their debut album went **platinum**.

LOUIS' GOT THE X FACTOR

Walsh became a **household name** in 2004 when he was hired as a judge on *The X Factor* alongside Sharon Osbourne and Simon Cowell. Walsh managed the 2004 *X Factor* runners-up G4 and 2005 winner Shayne Ward. Ward's debut single remained at Number One for four weeks and he has gone on to enjoy an international career. In 2008 Walsh **mentored** runner-up group JLS. Although he does not manage the group, he still provides them with support and advice in their increasingly successful career.

Walsh poses with Boyzone member Ronan Keating before one of the band's gigs.

CELEB BIO

Date of birth 5 August 1952

Place of birth Kiltimagh, County Mayo, Republic of Ireland

Bands Boyzone, Westlife, Jedward

Greatest achievement Creating two of the most successful boy bands of all time

'[The music industry's] a tough, awful business. But I love it.'

FACT

Walsh began his music manager career at the age of 15 with a heavy rock band called Time Machine.

THE SATURDAYS

'It's not necessarily about getting the jobs you audition for but meeting the right people in the process.'

VANESSA WHITE

Frankie Sandford, Mollie King, Una Healy, Vanessa White and Rochelle Wiseman (left to right) of The Saturdays perform at the Isle of Wight Festival.

Some bands are put together by record companies. They advertise auditions for 'the next big band' and select the members they want. These bands are called manufactured bands, because they have been specifically put together for the purpose of selling records.

AUDITION TIME

In 2007 record label Fascination Records (part of Polydor Records) wanted to **revive** the pop industry. Having already achieved incredible success with Girls Aloud, the label felt that a new girl band was the way to go and held auditions for members. The Saturdays were formed and have since become one of the UK's most popular girl groups.

PREVIOUS EXPERIENCE

All of the members had previous performance experience before auditioning. Friends Frankie and Rochelle auditioned together for S Club

Juniors and both became members of the band (which broke up in 2005). Una released a solo **EP** in 2006 called *Sorry*. Mollie auditioned for *The X Factor* as part of girl band Fallen Angelz and made it through to the boot camp stage. Vanessa went to stage school, and has performed in musicals including the London West End production *The Lion King*.

BEST OF FRIENDS

Band members have to work together 24/7, so it is very important that they get on with each other. The Saturdays were given time to **gel** as a band at the start and insist that they are now the best of friends. They have proven once again that manufactured bands can be successful – since their launch they have sold nearly two million records and scored eight UK Top Ten singles.

CELEB BIO

Date of birth **Una Healy 10 October 1981, Mollie King 4 June 1987, Frankie Sandford 14 January 1989, Rochelle Wiseman 21 March 1989, Vanessa White 30 October 1989**

Place of birth **London and Taunton, UK; Thurles, Republic of Ireland**

Albums *Chasing Lights* **(2008),** *Wordshaker* **(2009),** *Headlines!* **(2010)**

Achievements **Being invited to record the 2009 Comic Relief single**

www.thesaturdays.co.uk *And, if you like this... check out* **Cheryl Cole** www.cherylcole.com *and Girls Aloud* www.girlsaloud.co.uk

N-DUBZ

Dappy, Tulisa and Fazer have become one of the UK's most entertaining hip hop bands.

> 'Anything you want to do in life, you can do it. Drugs, guns, knives – stay away from it. I'm not who I am now through that – it's through my talent.'
>
> DAPPY

Some bands exhibit outstanding natural talent and an edge that makes them stand out from the crowd. British hip hop band N-Dubz have taken the music industry by storm with their talent, cutting-edge sound and unique image.

TOUGH START

N-Dubz members Dappy, Tulisa and Fazer all grew up in Camden Town in London. They had a tough childhood and were exposed to violence and gang culture during their teen years. Dappy and Tulisa are cousins and they met Fazer at school. When they were 13 they began performing together as a group, guided by Dappy's father who was a member of 1970s rock band Mungo Jerry.

ONWARDS AND UPWARDS

The trio released a couple of **underground** singles under the name 'Lickle Rinsers Crew' in the early 2000s, both of which became **pirate radio** hits. They briefly changed their name to NW1 (after the area in which they grew up) before settling on N-Dubz (a play on NW). N-Dubz self-released several early singles and built up a loyal fan base. In 2007 they turned heads when they won a **MOBO Award** for best newcomer without being signed to a record label.

LIVING THE DREAM

N-Dubz signed with dance label All Around the World in 2008 and have become one of the UK's most successful bands. They have collected four MOBO Awards and a Brit Award **nomination**. In 2010, N-Dubz achieved a dream when they signed with highly-regarded hip hop label Def Jam. As Def Jam is based in the USA, N-Dubz are looking forward to expanding their global audience and enjoying even more success.

FACT

Dappy and Fazer are said to have struggled to get a visa that will allow them to work in the USA because of their criminal convictions.

www.ndubz.com *And, if you like this... check out Roll Deep* www.rolldeepofficial.com *and Tinchy Stryder* starinthehood.net

15

THE WANTED

'Boy bands are taking over, but as long as we're all different and the music is good it doesn't matter how many there are.'

Devoted fans of The Wanted wait to meet them outside a book signing in Manchester, UK.

CELEB BIO

Date of birth Tom Parker 4 August 1988, Max George 6 September 1988, Siva Kaneswaran 16 November 1988, Jay McGuiness 24 July 1990, Nathan Sykes 18 April 1993

Place of birth UK and Ireland

Albums *The Wanted* (2010)

Achievements Their debut single went straight to Number One in the UK charts

Siva, Tom, Max, Jay and Nathan (left to right) **promote** their debut album.

FACT

Siva's sister appeared on reality TV show *Pop Stars: The Rivals*. She was dropped from the show and narrowly missed out on becoming part of Girls Aloud because she was 10 days over the maximum age limit!

Boy bands have always created fan hysteria. Many young lads dream of having thousands of screaming fans and living a celebrity lifestyle. For hot young boy band, The Wanted, this dream is a reality!

AUDITION TIME

The Wanted went from being unknowns to a seemingly overnight sensation when their debut single 'All Time Low' shot straight to Number One in the UK charts. However, before the release of the single, the band had spent weeks performing at schools and other **venues** around the country and visiting radio stations to promote the song. All of this helped to build up the **hype** around the band and develop a fan base before the single was released.

ALL ABOUT THE BOYS

The five members of The Wanted were put together following a mass audition. Jay is an amazing dancer and Nathan joined

the band straight from drama school. Tom once auditioned for *The X Factor* (but was unsuccessful) and loves playing the guitar. Max appeared on *The X Factor* as a member of boy band Avenue who achieved some chart success before splitting in 2009. Siva modelled from the age of 16 and was snapped up for the band due to his good looks (as well as his talent, of course).

ALL ABOUT THE MUSIC

The boys don't just have fantastic voices – they also get involved in songwriting and wrote about half of the music on their debut album. They have worked with a lot of popular producers and songwriters, including **R&B** star Taio Cruz, Cutfather and Cathy Dennis.

www.thewantedmusic.com *And, if you like this... check out Matt Cardle* www.mattcardlemusic.com *and Justin Bieber* www.justinbiebermusic.com

17

JLS

CELEB BIO

Date of birth Aston Merrygold 13 February 1988, Jonathan 'JB' Gill 7 December 1986, Oritsé Williams 27 November 1986, Marvin Humes 18 March 1985

Place of birth London, UK

Albums *JLS* (2009), *Outta This World* (2010)

Achievements Winning four MOBO Awards, two Brit Awards and three Urban Music Awards

The JLS members (left to right): Oritsé Williams, Aston Merrygold, Marvin Humes and Jonathan 'JB' Gill.

One of the most successful TV reality shows ever is *The X Factor*, which launches the careers of solo artists and pop bands. Loveable lad band JLS have been one of the biggest success stories to come from the show.

GETTING TOGETHER

Oritsé Williams wanted to put together the greatest boy band ever in order to raise money to find a cure for **multiple sclerosis** (his mother has the condition). He recruited Marvin Humes and Aston Merrygold, who impressed the lads with his gymnastic ability as well as his vocals. Last to join was JB, whose talent for **devising** harmonies gave the band a unique edge. The band named themselves UFO (Unique Famous Outrageous) and won an Urban Music Awards for Best Unsigned Act in 2007.

SHOW TIME

In 2008 they auditioned for *The X Factor*. As the name UFO was already taken, they settled on a new name – JLS (Jack the Lad Swing). JLS stood out with their tight vocals and cheeky attitude.

They cruised through the early stages of the show, developing a growing number of fans every week. The band eventually made it into the final and came runner-up to Alexandra Burke.

BEYOND *THE X FACTOR*

Since *The X Factor* JLS have enjoyed success after success. Most of their singles have reached Number One in the UK charts, their albums have been Top Ten hits (with *JLS* going platinum four times) and they have toured both the UK and the USA. Oritsé's aim of raising funds to help combat multiple sclerosis has become a reality. Despite being labelled 'the biggest boy band of a generation', the lads insist that they are keeping their feet firmly on the ground and concentrating on making great music for their fans.

TAKE THAT

Take That were one of the most successful boy bands of the 1990s. In 2006 they staged a startlingly successful comeback with the release of a new single and album, both of which topped the UK charts.

THE EARLY YEARS

Take That dominated the UK charts in the early nineties, with eight Number One singles and two of the best-selling albums of the decade. The band developed a huge following of fans in the UK, Europe and Asia (mostly female teenagers) and the BBC described them as 'the most successful British band since the Beatles'.

BAND BREAK UP

However, behind the scenes, tensions were mounting and Robbie Williams eventually left the band in 1995. Take That continued as a four-piece until February 1996 when the band announced that it was splitting up. Fans were devastated and the British government set up special **call centres** to support them!

BACK FOR GOOD?

A greatest hits album was released in 2005 and the band (minus Robbie) announced that they were returning to go on tour. The tour was a huge success, with tickets selling out within 30 minutes! The band enjoyed being back together so much that they decided to record a new album, *Beautiful World*, which went straight to Number One in 2006.

ROBBIE RETURNS

Following several Number One singles and another Number One album (*Circus* 2008), it was announced in July 2010 that Robbie Williams was rejoining the band. The *Progress* album was released and a 2011 tour, 'Progress Live' was announced. The tour broke all previous ticket sales records when it sold over 1.1 million tickets in just one day!

The fresh-faced members of Take That pose together at the very start of their career.

Jason, Howard, Robbie, Mark and Gary
(left to right) together again in 2010.

CELEB BIO

Date of birth **Robbie Williams**
13 February 1974, Mark Owen
27 January 1972, Gary Barlow
20 January 1971, Jason Orange
10 July 1970, Howard Donald
28 April 1968

Place of birth **Stoke-on-Trent,
Oldham, Frodsham, Manchester
and Droylsden, UK**

Albums *Take That & Party*
(1992), *Everything Changes*
(1993), *Nobody Else* (1995),
Beautiful World (2006), *The
Circus* (2008), *Progress* (2010)

Achievements **Winning seven
Brit Awards, two MTV Europe
Music Awards and one Ivor
Novello Award for songwriting**

'Being in a band again... You've got four other people with you that you can't let down and that you really want to impress.'

ROBBIE WILLIAMS

www.takethat.com *And, if you like this... check out Gary Barlow*
www.garybarlow.com *and Robbie Williams* www.robbiewilliams.com

SUGABABES

Heidi Range, Jade Ewen and Amelle Berrabah of the Sugababes perform together at the V Festival.

'We've got a lot of things to prove as a new line-up together, and we are just excited to get on with it.' HEIDI RANGE

When record labels put a band together they strive to find the best line-up possible, with a mix of looks, personalities and talents. The Sugababes has always had a unique look and sound, and they are the most successful female act of the 21st century according to *The Guinness Book of World Records*. Despite this success, the band has seen the line-up change a surprising number of times over the years.

The original Sugababes line-up consisting of Siobhán Donaghy, Mutya Buena and Keisha Buchanan.

STARTING OFF

The Sugababes was formed in 1998 with members Siobhán Donaghy, Mutya Buena and Keisha Buchanan. However, Donaghy decided to leave after the first album amid reports of fighting within the band, and former Atomic Kitten member Heidi Range was brought in to replace her. Childhood friends Buena and Buchanan are said to have made it hard for Range to settle in. However, she persisted and the trio released three albums together.

BUENA LEAVES

Throughout the years, the band has been **plagued** by reports of tantrums and infighting. This was fuelled further in 2005 when Buena left the group. She was replaced by singer Amelle Berrabah. Several tracks on the band's fourth album, *Taller in More Ways*, were re-recorded with Berrabah's vocals, and the album was re-released. Buchanan, Range and Berrabah then went on to make two Top Ten albums together.

BYE BYE BUCHANAN

Following the release of the **ironically**-titled album *Catfights and Spotlights*, the music industry was shocked when founding member, Keisha Buchanan, was dropped from the band in 2009. She was replaced by UK Eurovision contestant Jade Ewen. Despite now containing none of the founding members, the band's name survived and the new line-up released their album *Sweet 7* in 2010.

FACT

The Sugababes was the first girl band to achieve Number One in the UK singles, album, airplay and download charts at the same time.

CELEB BIO

Current members **Heidi Range Amelle Berrabah and Jade Ewen**

Date of birth **Ewen 24 January 1988, Berrabah 22 April 1984, Range 23 May 1983**

Place of birth **London, Aldershot and Liverpool, UK**

Previous members **Siobhán Donaghy (1998–2001), Mutya Buena (1998–2005), Keisha Buchanan (1998–2009)**

Albums *One Touch* (2000), *Angels with Dirty Faces* (2002), *Three* (2003), *Taller in More Ways* (2005), *Change* (2007), *Catfights and Spotlights* (2008), *Sweet 7* (2010)

Achievements **Winning one Brit Award out of six nominations, a Cosmopolitan Ultimate Women of the Year Award, a Smash Hits Award and receiving a MOBO Award nomination**

www.sugababes.com *And, if you like this… check out The Dolly Rockers* www.thedollyrockers.com *and Ke$ha* www.keshasparty.com/uk/home

BIFFY CLYRO

Simon, James and Ben of Biffy Clyro (left to right) hang out backstage before **headlining** at the RockNess Fesival in Scotland.

The buzz of a live performance, the roar of the crowd and the uncertainty of the weather all add up to make a festival one of the most exciting ways to perform music. Biffy Clyro love playing live and have been described as 'the UK's festival band'.

STARTING OUT

Biffy Clyro formed in Kilmarnock, Scotland in 1995. The band consists of lead singer Simon Neil and twin brothers James and Ben Johnstone. The band started off playing very small gigs in front of only a few people. Gradually news of their fiery live performances spread and their audiences and venues grew in size. In 2000 Biffy Clyro played the Unsigned Bands stage at Scotland's T in the Park festival and were spotted by a label **scout**. They were soon signed to independent label, Beggar's Banquet.

PLAYING LIVE

The band continued touring and performing live, but remained relatively unknown until the release of their fourth album, *Puzzle*, in 2007. The album shot straight to Number Two in the UK charts and was voted Best Album of 2007 by rock magazine *Kerrang!* That year, the band performed at several major festivals including Download, Glastonbury and the Reading and Leeds Festivals.

FESTIVAL FUN

Biffy Clyro have played most of the biggest festivals around the UK, including Edinburgh's Hogmanay Festival, the Sonisphere Festival in Knebworth, England, Irish festival Oxegen, V Festival in Staffordshire, England, and the Isle of Wight Festival. As an almost permanent fixture at T in the Park since 2000, fans have enjoyed tracking Biffy Clyro's performances and musical sound over the years.

'Just to get to stand in front of that many people and sing our songs, you know, that's the best thing... Truly nothing beats it.' SIMON

CELEB BIO

Date of birth **James Johnstone 25 April 1980, Ben Johnstone 25 April 1980, Simon Neil 31 August 1979**

Place of birth **Kilmarnock and Irvine, Scotland**

Albums *Blackened Sky* (2002), *The Vertigo of Bliss* (2003), *Infinity Land* (2004), *Puzzle* (2007), *Only Revolutions* (2009)

Achievements **Winning one Radio Teen Award, one *Kerrang!* Award and one *NME* Award**

FACT

The band hate being asked where the name 'Biffy Clyro' came from. If they are asked the question in interviews, they always make up a different silly story about the **origin** of the name. It is rumoured to be inspired by a Cliff Richard pen, or 'Cliffy biro'!

Lead singer Simon Neil performing at the iTunes Festival in London.

www.biffyclyro.com *And, if you like this... check out Mumford & Sons* www.mumfordandsons.com *and 30 Seconds to Mars* www.thirtysecondstomars.com

MUSE

'…we're pushing [the music] to new limits. Reaching new audiences. We've made more money than ever before!'

The members of Muse (left to right): Christopher Wolstenholme, Matthew Bellamy and Dominic Howard.

FACT

When Muse started making money, one of the first things Bellamy bought was a fully functioning jet pack!

Muse are one of the most famous and successful rock bands in the UK. Since their formation in 1994, they have grown in popularity and developed huge fan bases in countries around the world, including in Asia and North America.

SPECTACULAR PERFORMANCE

Muse have become well known for their incredible and intense live performances enhanced with over-the-top **props**, lighting effects and **pyrotechnics**. The 2010 tour featured lasers, a rotating platform that elevated above the crowd, an inflatable UFO and a somersaulting alien. Bellamy also dazzled fans in a sparkly-silver suit, followed by a flashing red version for the second **encore**!

MUSE-IC

Muse consists of Matthew Bellamy (lead vocals, piano and guitar), Chris Wolstenholme (bass guitar) and Dominic Howard (drums). The three met at college in the early 1990s and started writing music together. They tried out different names, such as Gothic Plague and Rocket Baby Dolls, before settling on Muse. The band has a unique rock sound and style – mixing heavy guitar **riffs** and electronic effects with classical piano and Bellamy's operatic **vibrato**. They have frequently been compared to 1970s rock legends, Queen, whose guitarist, Brian May, is a huge fan.

MAKING IT BIG

Since getting signed in 1998, Muse have released five **studio albums**, one **live album** and 26 singles. They have sold over 10 million albums worldwide and received almost 100 award nominations. Muse's unique rock sound and style has grabbed the attention of the music industry and fans alike.

CELEB BIO

Date of birth **Dominic Howard 7 December 1977, Matthew Bellamy 9 June 1978, Chris Wolstenholme 2 December 1978**

Place of birth **Stockport, Cambridge and Rotherham, UK**

Albums *Showbiz* (1999), *Origin of Symmetry* (2001), *Absolution* (2003), *Black Holes and Revelations* (2006), *The Resistance* (2009)

Achievements **Winning eight** *NME* **Awards, five MTV Europe Music Awards, five** *Q* **Awards, four** *Kerrang!* **Awards, two Brit Awards and one American Music Award**

Muse put on a show with an extravagant set and lighting effects at the Rock Im Park Festival in Nuremberg, Germany.

muse.mu *And, if you like this... check out Kasabian* www.kasabian.co.uk *and Green Day* www.greenday.com

GLOSSARY

audition A job interview for a singer, dancer or actor in which they have to perform to show their skill.

call centre An office in which large numbers of telephone calls are handled.

debut First.

devise To invent or make up.

encore An additional performance at the end of a gig in response to demand from the crowd.

EP A record that contains more tracks than a single, but not enough to qualify as an album. EP stands for extended-play.

fan base Collection of fans.

formula A method for achieving something.

gel To form a solid bond.

gig Another word for concert.

headlining When a band or artist is identified as the top act at a gig.

hooks Something that catches the listener's attention and is repeated throughout a piece of music.

household name Someone who is well known by the public.

hype Publicity to create excitement about something.

ironically Happened in way that is unexpected and amusing.

jet pack A device worn on the back which forces a stream of gases out of a small opening to give the user power to fly.

live album A collection of tracks that are recorded during a live concert and released as an album.

mentor To advise, support and train.

MOBO Award An award that gives recognition to an artist who performs music inspired by black people. MOBO stands for Music of Black Origin.

multiple sclerosis A disease in which the nerve cells in the central nervous system are damaged.

negotiate To make something happen through discussion.

nomination Chosen as a potential award winner.

origin The place or point when something started.

pirate radio An unofficial radio station.

plagued Constantly troubled or irritated.

platinum Describes a recording that has sold more than a million copies.

promote Help to create publicity for.

prop A portable object that is used on a stage (excluding furniture and costumes).

pyrotechnics Special effects that involve fireworks.

R&B Short for 'Rhythm and Blues'. A form of popular music with its origins in black American music.

record label A company that produces recorded music.

record producer Someone who supervises the making of a musical recording, responsible for turning the recorded sounds into a finished work.

recruit To persuade someone to join a group or organisation.

revive To give new energy to something.

riff A short repeated phrase in music.

scout Someone who searches for new talent.

studio album A collection of tracks recorded in the studio and released as a single item.

underground Not mainstream.

venue The place where something, for example a concert, happens.

vibe Feel.

vibrato A musical effect where the voice or instrument moves quickly between pitches, producing a richer tone.

BOOKS

21ˢᵗ Century Lives: Pop Groups by Liz Gogerly (Wayland, 2007)

21ˢᵗ Century Lives: Pop Stars by Liz Gogerly (Wayland, 2006)

Celeb: Pop Star by Clare Hibbert (Franklin Watts, 2010)

Celebrity Secrets: Pop Stars by Liz Gogerly (Wayland, 2011)

The Hip-Hop Scene: The Stars, the Fans, the Music by Ann Graham Gaines and Reggie Majors (Enslow, 2009)

The Story of Pop Music by Ben Hubbard (TickTock Books, 2009)

The Wanted: Me & You: The Unofficial Guide by Posy Edwards (Orion, 2010)

JLS: Another Beat by Posy Edwards (Orion, 2010)

WEBSITES

www.brits.co.uk
The official website of the BRIT Awards, the annual pop awards from the British record industry.

www.last.fm/music
Search the Last.fm website for profiles of your favourite artists.

www.mobo.com
The official website of the MOBO (Music Of Black Origin) Awards.

xfactor.itv.com
The official website for *The X Factor*.

Beatles, The 20
Biffy Clyro 24–25
boy bands 8, 10, 16, 17, 18, 19
Boyzone 10
Brit Awards 9, 15, 18, 21, 23, 27
Busted 8

charts 6, 17, 19, 20, 23, 24
Cowell, Simon 8

drummers 8, 9, 27

festivals 12, 22, 24–25, 27

gigs 6, 10, 24, 28
Girls Aloud 10, 13, 17
guitarists 8, 9, 17, 25, 27

hip hop 15

Ivor Novello Awards 21

Jedward 10
JLS 10, 18–19

Keane 6
Kerrang! Awards 24, 27

McFly 8–9
MOBO Awards 15, 18, 23
MTV Europe Music Awards 21, 27
Muse 26–27

N-Dubz 14–15
NME Awards 24, 27
Number Ones 6, 7, 8, 10, 16, 17, 19, 23

Q Awards 27
Queen 27

R&B 17, 28
record labels 8, 13, 15, 23, 24, 28
record producers 6, 17, 28
rock music 8, 11, 15, 24, 27

Saturdays, The 12–13
Scouting For Girls 6–7
singles 6, 7, 10, 13, 15, 16, 17, 20, 23, 27
Smash Hits Awards 9, 23
songwriting 8, 17, 27
Spice Girls 8
Sugababes 22–23

Take That 20–21
tours 19, 20, 24, 28

Urban Music Awards 18, 19

Walsh, Louis 10
Wanted, The 16–17
Westlife 10

X Factor, The 10, 13, 19